Fieldstones

Fieldstones

New Shoots from Stony Soil

by
Hearthstone

To the Gods.

Contents

Introduction.................10

Gods of Ireland.............12

Aengus..........................14

Aine..............................15

Airmed...........................16

Be Binn..........................17

Boann.............................18

Brigid.............................19

Cliodhna.........................20

The Dagda......................21

Danu..............................22

Dian Cecht.....................23

Donn..............................24

Eithne............................25

Etain..............................26

Fand...............................27

Flidais.............................28

Goibniu, Luchtaine, and

Creidhne.........................29

Lir..................................30

Lugh...............................31

Manannan mac Lir.......32

Medb..............................33

Morrigan........................34

Nuada............................35

Ogma.............................36

Tailtiu............................37

Gods of Wales.............38

Arianhrod......................39

Blodeuwedd...................40

Bran..............................41

Branwen.........................42

Cerridwen......................43

Gwydion........................44

Lleu Llaw Gyffes...........45

Mabon...........................46

Modron..........................47

Nimue............................48

Rhiannon........................49

Gods of Gaul & Britain.50

Abnoba...........................51

Alaunus..........................52

Alisanos..........................53

Ancasta...........................54

Andraste.........................55

Arduinna.........................56

Artio...............................57

Aveta..............................58

Belatucadros...................59

Belenos...........................60

Belisama.........................61

Bergusia.........................62

Borvo..............................63

Brigantia........................64

Camulus.........................65

Carantana.......................66

Cernunnos....................67
Cocidius.......................68
Coventina....................69
Damona.......................70
Epona..........................71
Erecura........................72
Esus.............................73
Etiona..........................74
Gnatus.........................75
Grannus.......................76
Hidua..........................77
Isosa............................78
Leucetius......................79
Lugus...........................80
The Matrones..............81
Meduna.......................82
Mogons.......................83
Mullo...........................84
Nantosuelta.................85

Naria............................86
Nehellenia....................87
Nemetona....................88
Nodens........................89
Ogmios........................90
Ritona..........................91
Rosmerta.....................92
Senuna.........................93
Sequana.......................94
Sirona..........................95
Sucellus........................96
Sulis.............................97
Taranis.........................98
Teutates.......................99
Ucuetis........................100
Vercana.......................101
Visucius.......................102
About the Gods..........104

Introduction

I grew up in the country, not far out of town but far enough. Always near large, unused fields, cleared long ago by farmers who had long since given up and moved on to something more profitable; our short growing season no doubt had something to do with this. So the fields were, and are, left ragged with bits of leftover hay growing among the long grass.

And often, in the middle of the field, there stands a large pile of rocks.

When I was a child, I didn't concern myself with how they got there. I just knew they were wonderful to climb and play on. I did sometimes wonder what might lie at the bottom–surely they must be covering some treasure, or perhaps some thing better left undisturbed, depending on which game we were playing that day.

What they actually were, though, was a bit less mysterious. Every spring, when the farmers prepared their fields, they found rocks that had not been there the previous year, driven to the surface by the winter. They would throw these rocks into a pile in the middle of the field, and after a few years this pile would be pretty big. (Back in those days, having a big pile of rocks in the middle of your hayfield was only a minor inconvenience; today's machines couldn't deal with it at all.)

The stones themselves, though, have a great deal of meaning to me, and not only because I am so fond of them. They also represent those pieces of the world that keep on surfacing, no matter what we do to move them to somewhere more convenient for us. They are persistent; they are insistent; and they never stop their progress.

Gods of Ireland

Aengus

I call to Aengus, fair-faced son of the Dagda,
son of deep-hearted Boann who knows the flow
of feeling, Aengus the young, Aengus the clever,
full-hearted god, child of love. Well you know the might
of words, you who slew the bard Abhean for his lies,
you who grant the sweetest speech to lovers and poets.
Well you know the worth of love, O seeker
of the swan maid; well you know the need of battle,
O bearer of Great Fury; Aengus Og were you called,
for the bloom of youth is ever upon you.
Dreamer of dreams, holder of hearts, mender of bones
and bodies, Aengus, I honor your complexity.

Aine

I call to Aine, child of the deep salt sea,
sister of fair Aillen of the burning breath,
mother of clans long-lived and far-flung,
taker of the might of kings, shining with the sun,
in times of old, on the shortest of nights
did bold fires burn 'til daybreak in your honor.
Aine, goddess, summer's dearest daughter:
the fields of golden grain, the deep green grass, flowing
with the wind, these are yours; the light of love
and the wrath of the wronged,
these too are in your realm.
Aine of the red mane, Aine of the black earth,
I praise your name, I honor your presence.

Airmed

Wise and gentle Airmed, whose art it is
to know the green things of the world, root and leaf,
stem and seed, to tend them with care, to work the soil
from which they draw their might; you hear each voice
of flower and weed, they speak to you of life and death,
of healing and of harm. Airmed, mender of men,
daughter of skillful Dian Cecht, whose wrath was borne
by your dear brother, you know the pain of a heart
torn by grief, you know the good of tears freely shed.
Airmed, beloved goddess, yours are the tonics
and balms that arise from the earth, yours the remedies
that ease body and spirit. Airmed, I call to you.

Be Binn

Gracious Be Binn, woman of strength, woman of worth,
O radiant one, of life's melody you know much.
Many are the tales told of you and yours, Be Binn;
many the bards who sought to sing of your beauty
and your courtesy, yet none could tell it true,
so fair you are, unbearably fair. Many too,
O goddess, the women of Eire who bore your name,
so strong the ties that bind you to that land.
You are with us when we enter this world, O goddess;
you are with us when we step into the next.
Be Binn, companion on our long, dear journey,
I seek your wisdom, I seek your blessing.

Boann

I call to Boann, goddess of the waters,
goddess of the ebb and flow, the power
of persistence, the gentle stream that makes its mark
on soil and stone alike. Beloved of the Dagda
who held the sun in place throughout your ripening,
throughout your travail, mother of fair Aengus,
born of love and treachery. Willful woman,
maker of the rushing river, swiftly you ran
from the surging well, fleet of foot; bearer of wounds
of body and of heart, you know that things of worth
may have their cost. Boann who looses the bonds
of knowledge, Boann of the white cow, I call to you.

Brigid

I call to Brigid, kind and clever goddess whose name
has never gone unspoken, whose gifts have never
gone ungiven. Brigid of the healing hands,
Brigid of the hammer and tongs, Brigid who sweetens
our words, who kindles the fire of poetry within us,
goddess to whom so many have turned in times
of joy and of desperation, who calms our fears,
who lights our lives, who warms our hearths:
O sisters three who hold all art and craft in hand,
Brigid of the flames,
O lady of comfort and good cheer, goddess dear,
I pray to you for understanding. Grant to me,
O goddess, the blessing of your presence.

Cliodhna

I call to Cliodhna of the Fortunate Isles,
daughter of the Danann, fair-haired Cliodhna
of the three bright birds that ate from the apple-tree,
their song a salve to any wound, any ill.
Pretty lovers you took, O goddess, mortal men
lured by your wondrous and terrible beauty,
yet ever did you return to the Land of the Young.
Cliodhna of the stony cairn, whose voice rang out
over hill and glen, a shriek to still the heart;
chief of the mound-women, chief of the mourners
of great men. Cliodhna of many guises,
I honor your story, I honor your name.

The Dagda

I call to you, O Dagda, mighty one, kindly one,
generous one, great god of many talents,
father of children good-hearted and strong,
master of treasures beyond telling, your cauldron
ever full, your trees ever heavy with sweet fruit.
Upon your oaken harp you play to bring the land
to new-grown life or set it to a winter's sleep;
in hand you wield the hefty club with which you take
or give back lives. O Dagda, god of many names,
granter of many gifts, holder of knowledge
and bearer of wisdom, worker of wonders,
you shield us in safety, you bless us with bounty.

Danu

I call to Danu, mother of the shining gods,
mother of children strong-willed and wise, goddess
whose power we know in rivers, in the flow
of time, whose shape we see in the curve of the hills.
From the sky came your far-famed kindred, O Danu;
to the land they traveled, to the sea they sailed,
within the earth they dwelt. Goddess of the waters,
goddess of the world, we say your name out loud
and hear it echo through the vales, through the years,
as if not a day had passed since first you trod
upon the stone and sod of Eire. Danu, goddess,
in bright skies and in mist I honor your might.

Dian Cecht

I call to Dian Cecht, who holds the strength of gods
and men in hand. Son of the good Dagda,
father of children sage and able, in you
do the suffering place their faith. Mender of bones,
easer of ills, the surgeon and the leech
seek your wisdom. Tales are yet told of the wonders
you have worked, of the blessed well Slane that heals
wounds grievous and grim, of the fair silver arm
borne by great Nuada. I pray to you, O knowing one,
share your gift of mind and body hale and whole,
more precious than all the world's treasures. Dian Cecht,
well-honored god, for me and mine I ask your favor.

Donn

Donn, first-born of the seven sons of Mil,
your father's father deep-rooted in the world,
Donn of the contrary tales, of the unwise words
to which peerless Eriu brought her wrath in answer;
as your brothers set their feet on the fair green isle,
you sunk into the sea. Upon the stony shore
you stand, on the isle of Tech Duinn; within the walls
of your great hall you make welcome those souls
who await their life's last journey, their passage
to the blessed isles to join their long-gone kin.
Kind one, bold one
whose blood yet runs in the veins of men,
O Donn of the fair folk, your children honor you.

Eithne

Eithne of the flowing hair, fair of face
and sweet of spirit, bright flame of life and hope
who shines forth in the dark, who endures in the storm.
Child of swift-striking Balor of the burning eye,
mother of Lugh whose wisdom and craft have no peer,
you know well the depth of sorrow and loss.
Daughter of the clan of Fomoire, a house old
and noble; bride you became to far-famed Cian
of the tribe of mighty Danu whose hand we yet see
on the good green land. Eithne called Feada,
queenly one, uniter of family, sustainer
of kin, I greet you with all reverence and honor.

Etain

Etain of whom great tales are told, most lovely of maids,
Etain the Horse Rider whose gentle hands
could guide the fiercest steed with ease,
Etain whose grace
never failed despite grief and misfortune,
I honor you, O lady, I honor your strength.
Unfortunate bride of Midir, great of heart
and great of love, who fondly named you Woman Fair;
silver-winged goddess, who suffered the wrath
of wronged Fuamnach; bride again, unlucky again,
of noble Eochaid. Etain of many sorrows,
Etain of many dooms, Etain of lives lived
with good intent and ill fortune, I honor you.

Fand

To Fand, fair Fand, I offer my praise. Goddess
of the cold blue sea, shining one, glorious one,
luminous as a perfect pearl, bittersweet
as a love long lost, pure as a sole salt tear,
I honor your ancient beauty, your depth of feeling,
your generous heart, O wise and knowing one.
Bride of Manannan, beloved of Cuchulainn,
woman of the otherworld, you know your worth,
you know your heart, your honor knows no compromise.
In all the worlds no woman is your equal,
O Fand of the distant isles; in all the worlds
no finer spirit may be found, O goddess.

Flidais

Flidais of the tangled wood, mistress of stag and doe
and all free creatures; Flidais of the flowing hair,
lovely one, changing one, bride of kings and mother
of champions, yours is the fair white cow that fed
the army of Connacht, yours the swift and sturdy
chariot drawn by wild-born deer,
your firm hand guiding
the skittish beasts with godly skill and certainty.
Mighty is your will that brings to rein the headstrong
and the mad, mighty your passion that sated
the lusty king of old Ulster. Flidais,
fierce one, gentle one, who follows no master,
who bears no constraint, I pray for your favor.

Goibniu, Luchtaine, and Creidhne

Goibniu of the hammer and the forge,
of the brawny arm and the answering strike,
maker of weaponry mighty and finely formed,
crafter of blades honed to a deadly edge,
brewer of the mead of invulnerability.
Goibniu, keen-eyed master of molten ore,
O god of art, blacksmith unequaled, I honor you.

Luchtaine of the knife and the supple tree,
of the skillful touch and the careful cut,
shaper of shields to hold back the fiercest foe,
craftsman who sees in the grain of any wood
the best and truest work that resides within.
Luchtaine, guide of the builder and the joiner,
O god of art, woodwright unequaled, I honor you.

Creidhne of craftwork delicate and defined,
molder of the metals of the deep earth,
who takes from craggy stone the glittering ore
and makes from it things of beauty and worth,
the choicest of treasures in any king's trove.
Creidhne, who knows the substance
within well-wrought work,
O god of art, goldsmith unequaled, I honor you.

Lir

Lir of the roiling sea, lord of the foam-flecked waves,
father of Manannan, father of the swan-children,
Lir of the lost tales, Lir called Allod of old,
I call to you. The realm of the deep is yours,
O ancient one, the waters that crest and crash
upon the coast; yours too is the might that guides
a ship to shore or pulls it down into the brine.
We know you in the cold salt spray, the icy wet
against our skin; we know you in the blood that runs
in our veins; we know you in the legacy
we share with all creatures who live upon the earth.
Lir who holds the essence of life, I honor you.

Lugh

I call to Lugh of the long arm, shining son
of bright-haired Ethne and Cian of ancient name,
child of compact, child of concord, child of clans
joined in might and in legend. Lugh of all skills,
master of all art and craft, ready with a sword
or with sweet speech, bearer of the far-famed yew,
many are the noble deeds, many the feats of strength
and spirit, many the perils faced, the battles fought,
the tales yet told of you, O Lugh. O clever one,
O cunning one, for any trouble you well know
the best solution, for any work you have
the talent, for any task you hold the tools.

Manannan mac Lir

I call to Manannan, free-flowing son of Lir,
keeper of the Blessed Isles, land of joy eternal,
land of the ever-young and the ever-fair,
land of the west, so far from the realm of men.
Ancient one, cunning one, tempter of Cormac,
scion of the sea, walker between the worlds,
guardian of the gates, cloaked in darkness,
wrapped in mist, master of magics, worker of illusion,
you veil the line between the seeming and the real.
Of you, O Manannan, are tales yet told; to you
is honor yet paid, on your dearest Isle of Man
and in lands that lie beyond the broad salt sea.

Medb

I call to Medb, bright-shining queen of ancient days,
heart of the land, holder of its right and its rule.
Your hand it was that made great kings,
that led great men
to fortune and to honor, to an undying fame;
your hand it is that leads us to know our worth,
to hold our heads high in weather fair or foul.
Gracious Medb, goddess most fair and most noble,
your glory unmatched, your words honey-sweet,
your presence at once a balm and a flame,
intoxicating one who shows us the way
to delight, in whom we may lose or find ourselves
in turn, I praise your name, I honor your might.

Morrigan

I call to you, O Morrigan, O awesome one,
O fearsome one, lady of the crow, goddess
of ancient name, of might beyond understanding.
In shape you shift, O goddess; in nature you endure,
you who stand alone in strength, you who are three,
who wears three forms, who bears three names:
Macha, Badb, Nemain.
Tester of heroes, holder of the land,
lover of great-hearted Dagda, firm of footing,
strong of arm, called on by those on fringe and frontier,
taker of the heart's blood, chooser of those who fall
in battle, you know well the fates of men. Goddess,
daughter of the Danann, I praise and honor you.

Nuada

I call to Nuada, first king of the people
of deep-hearted Danu, Nuada of the silver hand,
bearer of the bright-lit sword which no foe
can evade. Chieftain wise and brave, leader of men
in battle and in time of peace, master of the hunt,
fisher of fish, catcher of the beasts of the wood,
worker of magics, holder of knowledge deep
and wide, Nuada, you know of victory and of loss,
you know of power and of its lack;
you know of the obligation of sovereignty;
you know of the honor in struggle, the gift
of persistence. Nuada, I call to you.

Ogma

I call to Ogma, bearer of the speaking sword!
Persuasion is your gift, O god of discourse,
maker of the telling staves that bear your name.
In times of old were bards and poets held
in highest regard; their strength of wit was feared
by all, their wisdom and their learning sought
by chieftains and by kings.
The rhymer and the wordsmith
would seek your aid in ancient days, O Ogma,
that their words be made sweet, that their tongues
be made sharp, that their thoughts be made swift.
The singer and the scribe, the scholar and the sage,
all know your might, all hope for your favor.

Tailtiu

Great-hearted Tailtiu, daughter of distant kings,
beloved bride of Eochaid, enduring one
who lived through loss,
who weathered the storm of war
and stood strong in spite of sorrow and suffering.
Tailtiu, foster-mother of clever, crafty Lugh,
kind one who cared well for the long-handed one,
as if he were her own dear child; in gratitude
for your love and keeping, in honor of your goodness
and your mettle, did he decree that games be held,
that all should feast and frolic in your name,
recalling your virtue and your worth. O goddess,
Tailtiu of field and farm, I praise and honor you.

Gods of Wales

Arianhrod

Strong-willed Arianhrod, fair-faced sister of Gwydion,
daughter of the river-flow, mother of thrice-cursed Lleu
who met your challenges with courage and craft,
a proven man of worth and wisdom. Arianhrod,
your castle stands among green fields,
hewn from the stone below;
your castle stands among the stars,
bright-shining in the cold night sky. I call to you,
O bearer of the silvery wheel, cloaked in the darkness,
wrapped in the unknown; I call to you, O goddess
who knows the price of expectation, who knows
the dignity of the self, who knows the gravity
of the truth; I call to you with all reverence.

Blodeuwedd

White-fingered Blodeuwedd, maiden fair as the face
of the storm, you knew no mother's loving arms
nor father's strength to keep you safe; your life
was made to serve another's need. From flowers nine
your form was fashioned, of primrose and of broom,
of meadwort fresh and sweet,
of the chestnut and the bean,
of the sturdy oak and the tree of the may,
of the cockle that pricks and the nettle that stings.
Blodeuwedd, called faithless and wicked by those
who would profit by your being, you know much
of blame and betrayal, of a life with no recourse,
of choices made by a thorny heart–I honor you.

Bran

I call to Bran the Blessed, lordly one, raven-king,
son of Penarddun the beautiful, son of the sea,
brother of the white-winged one
whose heart broke of sorrow,
keeper of the marvelous cauldron of rebirth.
Bran of the battlefield, wise in the ways of war,
O chief of might and renown, great of glory.
Bran the open-handed, good and gracious host
of traveler and guest; your hearth is ever warm,
your table ever laden, heavy with food and drink.
The birds of the tower are yours, O Bran,
and the fine black earth beneath the stone.
To you I offer words of praise and reverence.

Branwen

Branwen of the Cymri, daughter of Llyr
of the darksome sea, daughter of Penarddun
called most fair, child of intrigue, child of hope,
sister of Bran called blessed, brave and true,
Branwen of the raven, a holy bird and wise,
Branwen whose tales are of grief and care, I call to you.
Goddess who knows much of shame and of sorrow,
of dignity and of betrayal, O woman wronged
and avenged, you know too the worth of honor
and its cost. Branwen of the mighty isle,
bride of the cruel king, friend of the mourner
and the shade, goddess, I praise and honor you.

Cerridwen

Beautiful Cerridwen, mistress of Awen,
holder of the vessel from which such insight flows,
friend of the poet, the rhymer, the bard,
I pray to you, I seek your blessing. Cerridwen,
keeper of the cauldron of wit and inspiration,
so deep, so sweet, so clear, so cold its waters!
Yours is a fount of change, a wellspring of becoming,
a draught of wisdom to quench the thirst of seeker
and sibyl, of scholar and stranger.
Cerridwen, strong-hearted goddess,
cloaked in wonder, wrapt in delight,
you know the worth of words,
you know the might of vision.
Cerridwen, goddess great and good, I honor you.

Gwydion

Gwydion, crafty and wise, master of the word,
master of the twists and turns of truth, I honor you.
Brother of the bear, child of the trees, Gwydion
who brought great Lleu into manhood by trickery
and wit, your guile and judgment know no equal.
Gwydion, strong of arm, stout-hearted in battle,
mighty of magic and terrible of power,
you know much of what is and what may be,
within the world and without it. Gwydion,
you know of transformation, of renewal
and return, of the line between loyalty
and necessity. To you I offer my praise.

Lleu Llaw Gyffes

I call to Lleu Llaw Gyffes, Lleu of the light,
Lleu of the darkness, Lleu of the three dooms.
Child of shining Arianhrod, borne away
and brought to manhood by crafty Gwydion,
brother of your mother;
bridegroom of the flower-maid,
bearer of the spear that pierced the stone,
of you such tales are told to stir the heart
and fire the blood! Lleu of the fine fair hair,
Lleu of the able arm, Lleu of mighty magics
who roused to battle the trees of the wildwood,
Lleu of the pledge upheld and the guileful word,
O great and glorious Lleu, I honor you!

Mabon

I call to Mabon, well-named son of Modron,
bright and glorious son of a blessed mother,
beautiful one, beloved child taken in the night.
O noble captive, Mabon of shackle and chain,
set free by the words of beasts wild and true
who knew well of your lodging and your lot;
Mabon of the strong arm and the sharp spear,
master of the horse and hound, best of huntsmen,
best of bowmen, swift of sword and fleet of foot,
your name known by many, your tales told by few,
shining and exalted god of tribes long scattered,
far-traveled. Mabon ap Modron, I honor you.

Modron

I call to Modron of the many faces,
Modron of deep roots and scattered seeds, Modron
mother of Mabon, mistress of field and harvest,
mistress of the river deep and wide, washer
at the shore, granter of the right of rule.
Modron of the dim-lit hill, subtle and enduring,
wise elder daughter of the faery king,
born to the isle of apple-trees, to a world
we see in shadows alone, a world we know
through the broken visions of poet and bard.
Modron, gracious goddess, friend of mother and child,
friend of the bereft, I praise and honor you.

Nimue

Nimue of the many names and the many tales,
of the deep and the dark, the many-layered well,
compassionate one who sits at the source of life,
lady of the blade and the sweet-water spring,
I call to you through the veil of the years,
through truths told in the space between words,
meaning made clear in the light within shadows.
Nimue, with time your stories dwindled,
your semblance grew less grand,
yet your substance and your strength endure.
Goddess, you come at moments desperate and dire,
O herald of the fatal day; you come to those
who act on faith alone. Nimue, I honor you.

Rhiannon

I call to Rhiannon of whom old tales are told,
Rhiannon of full fame, whose name is a melody,
whose spirit sings through the years,
through the hills and vales
of lands green and ancient.
From the fairy mound you rose,
O goddess, astride your dainty-footed steed,
your ramble seeming slow and yet so swift,
arrayed in fine silks, well draped in bright gold,
a fairer figure never stood upon the sod.
Rhiannon of legends, Rhiannon of sorrows,
you know of betrayal, you know of the heart's loss,
you know of the will to seek the right and the true.
Peerless goddess, noble and wise, I honor you.

Gods of Gaul & Britain

Abnoba

I call to Abnoba of the wilderness,
your bow at the ready, your well-honed shafts at hand;
keen of eye you are, goddess, and fleet of foot,
your nerve never falters, your aim never errs.
Abnoba who we see in the shift of shadows,
whose breath we feel on the back of the neck,
we hear you in the cry of the hawk, the bay of the wolf,
we know you in the tangled wood,
the cold-water stream,
the sweet scent of fallen leaves in decay.
The madness of the hunt is yours, O goddess,
the pounding heart of predator and prey;
Abnoba of the shining eyes, I honor you.

Alaunus

Gracious Alaunus, well known in the heart of Gaul,
god of the healing hand who knows well the ways
of staunching a free-flowing wound, of mending
broken flesh and bone, of cooling a fevered child;
god of the small voice that speaks in dreams and visions,
I call to you. Alaunus, granter of concord
among comrades, of amity among strangers,
of understanding among clan and kin,
your favor falls on those who seek the commonweal,
your wrath on the thief and the swindler. Alaunus,
god of the honest and the honorable,
the open-handed and the good, I praise you.

Alisanos

Alisanos of the tree and the stone,
of the mountain and the wood, I call to you.
God of the golden hills, of the spring and the vine,
granter of what is needful, what is pleasant
in life, you know the worth of the moment,
you know the strength of small things,
the might of one man
and the greatness of many standing steadfast,
working in unity. O constant one,
O god whose works and legends lie in shadow,
Alisanos in whom folk once placed
their trust, their faith,
Alisanos whose blood and bone are of the earth,
I seek understanding, I offer you my praise.

Ancasta

Ancasta of the rushing river, Ancasta
of the fair white feet, laughing you leap from stone
to slippery stone, each step a dance of grace and ease.
Carefree one, unwavering one, we hear your voice
in the music of the rapids, we find your gifts
in the taste of good sweet water on our tongues,
in the silvery glint of salmon and trout
among the rocks and mosses. Your might was great
in days long past, your kindness and your bounty;
your name was carved with grateful hands
by one who knew your blessing,
who prayed to you with love and faith.
Ancasta, goddess, ancient one, I honor you now.

Andraste

Shining Andraste, great of glory, great of name,
most noble of goddesses, in you did the mighty
place their faith of old. Andraste of the Iceni,
in desperate times did bright-haired Boudicca
call on you, and neither she nor you will ever
be forgotten. Andraste of the blood-stained field,
swift-riding goddess of honor and strife,
invincible mistress of contest and conflict,
friend of all those who struggle for the right,
I call to you. Andraste, you know that in this life
victory goes oft not to the good but to the strong,
and yet such a battle is well worth the fighting.

Arduinna

Lovely Arduinna, lady of the forest,
of hill and of mountain, I offer you my praise.
Graceful goddess of the wild whose firm hand
and gentle voice make tame the savage boar,
sharp of tusk and fierce of spirit; upon the back
of the baleful beast you ride, with neither fear
nor trouble to hinder your journeying.
Fair is the land of your people, Arduinna,
high-peaked and deep-valed, with rivers swift and stony.
The beasts of the wood are yours, O goddess,
and those who hunt in your domain must pay your fee.
Arduinna of famous name, I call to you.

Artio

Artio, goddess, bold of spirit, strong of heart,
fair one, gracious one, queen of the wilderness,
mistress of bears, I call to you this day.
Gentle goddess, you face without fear the greatest
of beasts, unarmed and ungirded you enter
the den; in hand you hold the fragrant blossom,
in arm you bear the finest fruit, ripe and ready,
honey-sweet as when it was plucked from the tree.
Artio, mountain-goddess, through tangled wood
and stony stream you run, fleet of foot and graceful
of carriage, firm of will and noble of bearing.
Artio, long-beloved goddess, I honor you.

Aveta

I call to Aveta, lady of sweet water,
holder of that which is good and pure, of that
which brings life to the world, of that which nourishes
and sustains us. Aveta, comforter of parents,
best of midwives, best of nurses, in your arms
you hold the newborn babe, in your arms you enfold
the fearful new mother, sharing with her
your strength and your wisdom. Kind-hearted Aveta,
friend of the little ones, friend of those who sit up late
and rock the cradle, who sing softly and endlessly
while babies fuss and fret, goddess, I thank you
for so many blessings, for your most precious gifts.

Belatucadros

I call to Belatucadros, light of the mere,
friend of those who count their wealth in copper coins,
who know the worth of a loaf of bread
when winter comes.
Long ago your name was carved in red, spoken
by those who held the line, who trod in the mud,
side by side with their fellows, their friends, their kin.
Beautiful in battle, beautiful in the hunt,
you wear the ornaments of war, the sharpened shaft,
the bloodied blade; you hold in hand the lives of men,
to scatter afield for the raven's feed
or set aside for another season.
Belatucadros, ancient one, I honor you.

Belenos

Belenos of the bright-lit sky, shining forth
between the clouds,
I praise your presence and your name.
From the blue southern seas to the snow-tipped Alps
to the storied isles of Britain, well-known you were
to those who walked the green sod of Gaul. Belenos,
shining one, your shrines stood strong across the land;
many were the gifts given you by the faithful
and the thankful, pretty things carved in oak and stone,
sweet fruit and cakes; many were the blessings granted
to the ailing and the desperate. Kind-hearted one,
protector against plague, god of merry May,
I offer you all honor and reverence.

Belisama

I call to Belisama, lady of light,
lady of fire, of the swift-rushing river
and the depths of the tranquil lake. Belisama,
when the sun is high and the days are long,
when stone and sod are warm against our feet,
we feel your might. Belisama of the grove,
once well known in Britain's green and flourishing hills
and in the ancient lands of Gaul, Belisama
of the temple and the wildwood, honored
when the sun is strong, recalled with love and longing
when the winter winds bluster and howl, O goddess,
Belisama, summer-bright, I offer you my praise.

Bergusia

Great-hearted Bergusia of long-lost Alesia,
deep within the golden hills of Burgundy,
I call to you. Bergusia of the burnished blade,
lady and beloved of peerless Ucuetis
of fire and forge, keen of eye and firm of will,
you share his temples and his craft. Bergusia,
whose gift it is to bring beauty to all the works
of skillful men, whose blessings fall on the honest
and the diligent, who rewards hard work and care
with fair return and good repute, friend of the smith
and the artisan, you lend your strength and vision
to those who hold your art in hand.
Goddess, I praise you!

Borvo

Borvo of the healing spring, Borvo of the river
and the well, all through the broad lands of old Gaul
were you well known, well honored by those in need;
many were the offerings made to you by the hopeful
and the thankful, many the blessings received
by those who placed their faith in you, O god
of remedy and relief. Borvo who soothes all hurts,
Borvo of the roiling waters,
the frothy waves that surge and whirl,
the seething pools that ease our pains,
consort to Damona of the great kind eyes,
Borvo who dwelt in many places, who answered
to many names, I pray to you, I praise your might!

Brigantia

Excellent Brigantia, goddess on high,
kind one, strong-minded one,
whose lands spread far and wide,
whose temples are long fallen into the deep earth,
whose name yet endures,
whose hand yet works upon the world.
Many were the tribes of old that placed their faith
in you, O goddess; your might a refuge to the weak,
your touch a salve to the ailing and afflicted,
your blessing sought by those in need, your favor
granted freely to good and honest folk.
Brigantia, mistress of the peak and the moor,
mistress of the river flow, the crest and the crown
are yours; I call to you, goddess, with words of praise.

Camulus

Camulus of the oak leaf and the ram,
warder of the battlefield, master of war
and all its arts, granter of strength and will
to those who follow your calling, I salute you.
In high lands and in low, from Britain's northern bounds
to the wilds of great Gaul, your might was well known,
your name carved deep in stone
by those who put their faith
in you; many were the prayers said to you
for courage and for victory, for refuge
and salvation. Our fathers of a thousand years
and more made offering to you, O Camulus;
hear our call, O god of the one and the many.

Carantana

I call to Carantana, unwavering one,
constant friend of all who seek your blessing,
beloved of your people, firm-footed of stance,
steady of gaze, true of course and certain of resolve.
Carantana of the marsh and the wood,
goddess who has seen the fall of kings and princes,
who has watched as empires crumble
and fade; Carantana,
who knows that a small creature may hold a great soul,
who knows that the good within mankind overmatches
the ill, who knows what must die and what must endure.
Goddess, granter of a full heart, a wise spirit,
a will strong and supple, I praise and honor you.

Cernunnos

I call to Cernunnos of ancient bearing,
enthroned in the splendor of moss and stone;
all creatures of earth and air lay at your feet,
taking comfort and shelter in your presence.
Cernunnos of Gaul, Cernunnos of the scattered tribes,
O god of field and forest, broad-antlered one,
bearer of the shining torc, hidden by the years,
shadowed by leaf and branch, friend of the stag and doe,
granter of good, for a full purse and a full belly
we thank you. Cernunnos, lord of the wildwood,
vigor and vitality you gift to man and beast;
for all your blessings, all your works, I honor you.

Cocidius

I call to Cocidius of the northern wood,
bearer of spear and shield, chaser of man and beast,
beloved of the soldier and the huntsman.
Cocidius, yours were the people of the deer,
of the thick-grown meadow and the wildflower field;
you watched as the men of Hadrian dug in the dirt
and lay the silty stone, as time and again
the good green land was taken. Cocidius
of the alder tree, honored in sheltered grove
and simple shrine, your image shaped in stone,
carved in thanks by hardened hands, Cocidius,
I offer you my words of reverence and praise.

Coventina

Coventina, lady of the deep waters,
well-revered in ancient days, goddess of the north,
your people journeyed far in the wide world,
carrying with them your name and their trust.
Many were the offerings made into your well,
many the prayerful words, spoken with feeling,
spoken with faith, many the coins and rings
and pretty things, given you in thanks for your blessings.
Lovely one, gracious one, guardian of travelers,
healer of ills, you know the good of cool, clear water,
you know the need of men and women for comfort
and for sustenance of soul. Goddess, I honor you.

Damona

Damona, lady of the sparkling rivers,
the seething springs that ease the ache of flesh and bone,
that soothe the souls of the weary and the wounded,
I call to you, O friend of the suffering.
Fair Damona, crowned in corn, merciful one
who so many have turned to for healing and relief,
in times long gone they spoke your name in prayer,
carved it in stone in thanks for your blessings;
still you grant your gifts to those who gather
at your temple, who bathe in your warm waters.
Deep-eyed goddess, good of heart and great of spirit,
with reverence I speak your name, I ask your favor.

Epona

Far-faring Epona whose goodness and grace
are well known, whose name was called out in prayer
across the broad lands of the old world, Epona
of Gaul and of Rome, Epona of the mare
and the foal, goddess enthroned, I pray to you.
Epona, goddess wreathed in roses, bearer
of fruit and golden grain, granter of blessings
needful and dear: by your might, O Epona,
wild horses grow gentle, barren fields become green,
famine and drought submit to your will. Epona,
goddess whose honor and renown yet grows,
I offer you my praise and my devotion.

Erecura

Great-hearted goddess, Erecura of field and vale,
Erecura who knows the warmth of sod and soil
on bare feet, who knows the light of the noonday sun
and the gentle dark of the life beyond life.
I call to you, Erecura, mistress of the earth,
of the seeds we plant in the good black ground,
of the graves we dig in the dirt and the clay,
gracious one, merciful one who is our guide
through all our life's long journey, who is our friend
in times of joy and sorrow. Erecura, bearer
of the bountiful horn, you gladden our spirits,
you comfort our souls; I praise and honor you.

Esus

I offer praise to Esus, god of fearful might,
healer of ills, granter of good, holder of lives.
Esus of the bull and crane, Esus of the axe,
well honored by the Treveri, well known throughout
the lands of Gaul, your image carved in stone,
your name preserved a thousand years and more.
Giver of blessings dark and bright, in days long gone
your altars stood, red-stained and worn
in fields of green; in days long gone
your tales were told, your name called out
in prayer and in thanks; your stories are lost to us,
O Esus, yet your name remains and is enough.
Esus of the willow-tree, I honor you.

Etiona

Etiona of the hazel tree, of the center,
heavy and sweet, of the slick smooth stones that line
the river-bed, green with persistent life,
I call to you. Etiona, O goddess fair,
holder of the heart of wisdom, who knows the pleasures
of understanding, the worth of insight,
the riches that lie in the words of wise women
and learned men. Your gift it is to find
what is hidden, to bring light to what is dark,
to take joy in puzzles and riddles, to question
all things and to seek all answers. Etiona,
granter of curiosity and of the wit
to wield it, I honor you and ask your favor.

Gnatus

Gnatus of lore and learning, fair of face,
noble of bearing, bright-eyed with wit and reason,
Gnatus whose shrine stood in the heart of Gaul,
in a land carved by riverflow, a land of farms
and pretty villages, where once the wise made offering
to you, I honor your name, I honor your work.
All of sense and judgment is yours, O great god
who sees what is and what may be. Gnatus,
granter of the might of knowledge, the moment
of revelation, the flow of understanding,
the spark of inspiration, the surge of spirit
that makes thought into substance, I call to you.

Grannus

Grannus of the seething springs, the healing baths
of far-famed Gaul, so long ago your might was known,
so many thousand-years ago your glory shone
upon the land. You know well of the faith of men,
your name called out in heartfelt prayer,
carved deep in stone,
acclaimed by those who knew your gifts, the pious
and the supplicant. You know well of the faith of men,
so fleeting and so fervent, so strong it yet abides,
in the fiery sheaf, in the ten-night feast.
Grannus, granter of wellness to the ailing,
mender of bones broken and hearts torn asunder,
I call to you with reverence; I offer you my praise.

Hidua

Great-hearted Hidua of the green fields of Gaul,
your feet firm-planted in the sun-warmed soil,
your hands, strong and skillful, in the good black earth,
I call to you with words of joy and good cheer.
Hidua whose gift it is to bring forth life,
who knows the pain of women in their travail,
who eases the passage of the new-born babe,
I call to you with words of prayer and thanks.
Hidua who knows that each journey
has within it an end, who knows that each door
has beyond it a path, who knows much of hope,
I call to you with words of remembrance and praise.

Isosa

Excellent Isosa, unsurpassed goddess,
worthy of all honor, all glory, all praise.
In times long gone you held the faith of many,
you bore the trust of those in need, of those who knew
your blessings; they called to you in love and prayer,
in times of joy and sorrow. Isosa, gracious one,
your name so long unspoken,
your hymns so long unsung,
your stories lost to time, your temples fallen to dust,
and yet a mighty name you bear, a promise
rooted in the earth, a pledge preserved by blood.
Isosa, I offer you words of reverence;
I stand before you in wonder and in awe.

Leucetius

Great Leucetius, light of the clouded sky,
light of the stormy night, I honor you.
God of the firebolt, warder of the world,
your might was once well known across the broad lands,
your name a word of power, spoken with love
by those who knew your blessing,
shouted out by soldiers
as they entered the field of battle, whispered
in hope and desperation by mothers sitting
in the dark with a sick child. Your fame has faded,
Leucetius, but your light has never dimmed,
your strength never faltered, your care never wavered
for those under your protection. Great one, I praise you!

Lugus

To wide-ranging Lugus I offer my prayer.
O god of many, ever are you with your people,
warding the home or watching over the traveler;
ever do you grant your gifts to the artist
and the tradesman, the maker and the warrior.
Noble Lugus, consort of shining Rosmerta,
from the dark you arose, O wise one, O clever one;
from your hands fall bright gold,
the reward of the worthy,
given to those whose craft and toil bring into being
works both useful and fair. Well known you were
in Gaul and in Galicia, O thrice-honored god;
I honor you this day, O Lugus, O constant one.

The Matrones

I call to the Matrones, mothers three,
mothers of old, mothers of us all! Kind ones,
gentle ones, your blessings were known to many tribes,
in many lands; when fortune carried your people
to strange places, you guided their travels,
you guarded their repose. Mothers three, mothers
of our foremothers, I pray to you as did
those women whose blood runs in my veins, I pray
with a full heart, in a voice soft with love,
a voice rich with the resonance of the years.
O you midwives, nurses, bearers of bounty,
goddesses great and gracious, I honor you.

Meduna

I call to Meduna of the patient vale,
Meduna of the tangled vine, the crimson fruit,
the gift of the single-minded bee, the drink
of poets and of kings. Meduna of transcendence
and of fury, of madness and delight, goddess
honey-sweet and fair, a joy to men and women,
a breath of inspiration, a goad to those who strive.
Meduna of the red hills and the riverside,
of the land that holds tight to memory,
that coils its roots with earth and stone,
in days long lost your image stood in stone,
worn smooth by prayerful hands;
this day I offer you my reverence and praise.

Mogons

I call to Mogons, leader of men, protector
of the people, friend of those who serve the good
of all, who offer their strength and their spirit
for the sake of hearth and kin. Upholder of honor,
companion of the worthy and the righteous,
in far-flung lands your altars stood, carved in rough stone
by those who knew your favor, raised up in hope
and thanks by those who trusted you with their lives.
Mogons, great of the battlefield, great of the hunt,
you hold the might of many in each heavy hand.
Mogons, champion of those who struggle and strive,
god to whom all works are possible, I praise you.

Mullo

I call out to Mullo of the healing hand,
O gracious one whose art it is to clear the eyes.
Your temples stood of old in great Gaul, in the land
of the north-men, in the land of standing stones
and icy waters. Mullo of the river-fork,
god of the mound and the sanctuary,
friend of the injured and the invalid,
the suffering and the sick, your shrines once held
hope for the ailing, who offered their prayers to you
with love and faith; your might is yet a boon to men,
your kindness a balm to body and spirit.
Mullo who brings light into darkness, I honor you.

Nantosuelta

Gracious Nantosuelta, holder of the home,
abundance is your blessing, contentment is your gift.
Well-crowned goddess, draped in fine raiment,
garlanded in gold, in you we see the riches of the world.
We know you, goddess, as we know honey
on the tongue, as we know warm grass on bare feet;
you are as heady, goddess, as the sweet new wine.
The dove is yours, Nantosuelta, white as milk,
fragile and free; yours too, O goddess, is the raven,
yours too the way of that coal-black bird. Nantosuelta,
in arm you bear the plentiful horn, in hand you grasp
the chalice; for your gifts I honor you, O goddess.

Naria

Naria of the bright eyes and the flowered fields,
lady of green meads and fair fortune, I praise you.
Long ago your people walked the heavy-wooded land;
sheltered by stone, they stood on the bank
of the uneasy Thielle and watched the waters
fall and rise. Well-crowned goddess, draped in raiment
rich and comely, gracious goddess who answers
the prayers of the pious, of those who pledge their faith
to you; Naria of the orchard and the vine,
granter of the blessings of the earth, the gift
of happy chance, of counsel close and deep,
I honor your kindness, I honor your might.

Nehellenia

Fair Nehellenia, you stand by the sea,
by the shore; friend of the sailor and the voyager,
friend of those in need, your altars stood strong
by the broad blue Rhine and the north sea-coast.
Gracious goddess, on many stones your form was carved,
with kindly face and arms well filled with crusty bread
and apples, at your feet a hound of gentle mien.
In days less ancient, goddess, were you unknown
to men, your might and goodness long forgotten;
yet still you stood, still you held the sea as your own,
'til your name came back to the world
by wind and by rain.
Nehellenia, goddess of old, I honor you.

Nemetona

Nemetona, goddess of green groves,
who hallows the good earth beneath our feet,
the stones within the soil, the tall trees rooted
in dirt and clay, seeking the sweet water
far below--all grow in spirit and substance
at your touch. Queenly one,
well crowned, well enthroned,
your grace and might well known in times long past,
O far-famed goddess, your name a prayer of sanctity.
Nematona, guide me to stand firm-footed and free
in the warm grass, guide me to feel the coming cold
underneath me, help me to know the sacred world
around me. Goddess, I praise you and ask your blessing.

Nodens

Excellent Nodens, master of the shining sea,
rider of tide and bore, who stands upon green hills,
whose will it is that tribe and village flourish,
fortunate are those you favor, fruitful their fields,
gainful their efforts, successful their battles;
their families thrive, their larders fill, all by your might
and goodness. We see your hand in all the games
in which we hold a stake–in combat and commerce,
in hunting and healing, O Nodens the catcher,
who brings food to the table, who wards against all ill.
Nodens of ancient name, friend of those who live
in a hard world, I call to you, I ask your blessing.

Ogmios

Ogmios of the nimble wit, of words well-chosen
and judgment fine and shrewd, with chains of gold
through your skillful tongue that hold the mortal mind
enthralled; sun-browned Ogmios, strong of arm
and wise beyond the years of men, bearer of the bow
and the knotted club; Ogmios the persuader,
granter of the gift of gab, master of wordplay,
friend of the chieftain and the bard, I call to you.
Ogmios, you know that strength of word and will
can prevail where thew and sinew come to naught;
you know the power of speech, the rhetor's craft
and the poet's fire. Ogmios, I praise your name.

Ritona

Ritona of the river-ford, who knows the flow
of time and might, lady of the Treveri
who held the wooded lands of Gaul, whose name
and honor yet endure, whose children's children
yet flourish. Protector of household and village,
your temples stood in times now gone, built with skill
and care by those who knew
your goodness and your gifts.
Joyful one who loves the merriment of life–
the laughter of children at play, the festival
and feast, the song and dance and telling of tales–
all are yours, O Ritona of the waterway.
Goddess, I speak your name in reverence and praise.

Rosmerta

Beloved Rosmerta, blessed one, bringer
of prosperity, provider of plenty,
giver of gold and guardian of grain, goddess
beneficent, goddess benevolent,
friend of the deep earth, friend of wayward fortune,
I honor you, I honor your might. Rosmerta,
long ago your temples stood across the land,
your image carved with care in stone or cast in bronze,
holder of the harvest horn, bearer of the bowl;
your presence, O goddess, makes all places holy.
Shining Rosmerta, receiver of offerings,
receiver of faith, I pray to you for favor.

Senuna

I call to Senuna, so good and so fair,
lady of the chalky spring, your waters steady
and pure, lady of the thick-grown wood. Senuna,
whose ancient shrine once grew a prosperous town
to which the faithful traveled long ago. Senuna,
your name once lost to man, a thousand-year and more.
In times gone by you received such offerings–
shining coins of silver and gold, rings and chains
of delicate grace, jewels and adornments
that glitter and gleam–all given you by those
who knew your blessings. Senuna, goddess returned,
I praise you with words of reverence and awe.

Sequana

Sequana of the springs, of water good and sweet,
Sequana of the river-mouth, the fabled Seine
that gives life to the land, goddess whose gentle arms
hold the wounded and the ill, bringing healing
and comfort to those in need, I call to you.
Many were the offerings, finely-crafted figures
of silver and bronze, given you in thanks and praise.
Many were the women and men who by your will
and kindness lived lives long and filled with happiness.
Sequana, bright-crowned goddess,
of health and wholeness
you know well; O granter of strength and vigor,
I honor your goodness, I honor your might!

Sirona

Sirona, soft of voice and gentle of hand,
whose bright eyes we see in the star-scattered sky,
I call to you. Goddess of the broad blue river,
goddess of the sulfurous spring, Sirona,
your name was spoken in prayer so long ago
by the ailing and the injured, with thanks to you
they poured out the sweet wine of the valley;
we say your name again this day with reverence
and awe. Sirona, easer of ills, healer of wounds,
mender of bones, soother of souls, you restore us
to wholeness, you bring us back to ourselves.
Sirona of the serpent, I honor your good works.

Sucellus

Great-hearted Sucellus, open-handed god,
beloved of bountiful Nantosuelta,
strong-armed one, friend of the farmer and the smith,
for a good life we thank you, O god of simple
joys and pleasures. Sucellus of the hammer,
good striker, granter of blessings dear to all men,
master of the grape and the rich red wine,
you take in hand the golden grain and turn it
to bitter ale; for the gift of ease and ecstasy
we thank you. In ancient days were you well honored,
Sucellus of field and forest, given prayer
and offerings; this day I honor you once more.

Sulis

I call to Sulis of the good land, of gentle hills
and apple trees, whose kindness is constant,
whose hand we see in budding branches
and rich harvests.
Sulis of the fair green vale, Sulis of the springs,
long has your name been spoken by those in need,
long have men and women sought your blessings,
long have you granted the gift of health and wholeness
to those who entered your temple, to those who bathed
in your healing waters, to those who prayed for respite
or remedy. Gracious mother of Somerset,
mender of ills, righter of wrongs, foe of the thief
and the villain, Sulis, I offer words of praise.

Taranis

I call to Taranis, master of the rumbling sky,
who holds the fearful thunderbolt and hurls it
with full force, with a true eye and a strong arm
you grant this gift. You send the havoc of the storm
to earth, you send as well the life-giving rains,
the lightning that gives breath to the soil. Taranis,
sky-god, the wheel of the sun is yours;
in times long gone your people held it
as a token of your might,
keeping it close when all was well, clutching it tight
in desperate hours. Across the broad plains, within
the deep wood, so long ago your name was known,
was spoken in prayer--I speak it now, O ancient one!

Teutates

Teutates of the far-flung clans, Teutates
of the people, great one who holds together
those who are bound by blood, by name, by those
who have gone before us and those yet to walk
upon the earth, I call to you with the voice
of my mothers, my fathers, my kin of years long gone;
I call to you with the voice of those who held you dear,
O god who knows each new babe born,
who knows each from their first sharp breath
'til the last beat of their heart.
Mender of fences, builder of bridges, you find
the lost and bring them home again; Teutates,
shelter of the family, shield of the tribe, I praise you.

Ucuetis

Ucuetis of the hammer and tongs, strong of arm
and sure of strike, god of forge and furnace,
master of the anvil's art, I offer you my praise.
Ucuetis, in times long gone you heard the prayers
of those whose work it is to arm the soldier,
to shoe the horse, to make bright gold and stone
into treasures to adorn a queen's smooth throat
or enrich a king's hoard. Your temple stood,
Ucetius, beneath the crafters' hall, the sound
of sledge on iron ringing out, a wordless hymn.
Lord of the uncertain lands, lord of the smithy,
shaper of men and of metal, I honor you.

Vercana

Vercana of the open heart, goddess wise and good,
so great of might, so intricate of calling,
whose works brought ample blessings to the children
of men, I call to you. Gracious Vercana,
who knew the Treveri who held the rolling hills,
who knew the artisans of Rome who built the baths
of Bertrich, who hears the prayers of the sick
and the desolate, who grants voice to the poet
and will to the wronged. Vercana of the scalding spring,
granter of insight, granter of vision,
granter of fire and fury, singer of the war-song,
shield of frail humanity, I honor you.

Visucius

I call to good Visucius of the borderland,
god of the black bird, god who knows. Visucius,
once you were well honored along the broad blue Rhine,
its waters sweet and cold; so many battles fought,
so many fortunes won and lost, fortresses raised
and ruined, all in your domain, O god who watches
the waterway. Visucius of the swift river,
friend of the merchant and the peddler, whose hands
are filled with coins of bright gold, who guides the flow
of fortune, I offer you words of reverence
and praise. Visucius of the vine-covered hills,
gracious and merciful one, I honor you.

About the Gods

Most of the information on the gods of Ireland and Wales is from various myths, so details can vary depending on the source; particularly in the case of Wales, mythological characters are not always identified as deities, possibly due to the stories having been written down in the post-Christian era. I am taking the broad view here and using the words "goddess" and "god" to refer to these supernatural entities.

Most of the information on the gods of Britain and Gaul, on the other hand, is archaeological or historical, a circumstance that provides its own challenges including the tendency of the Roman writers to equate all gods with their own. As a polytheist, I see each deity as unique, something I hope comes through in this book; it's not a matter of theology, it's a matter of practicality and what seems to work.

The Celtic gods did not comprise a pantheon in the sense that the Greek or Roman gods did--most of these deities were associated with specific tribes and/or regions, and would not have been worshiped together traditionally unless they both came from the same region, and possibly not then.

Also please note that these descriptions are intentionally very brief and minimal; I've listed names, locations and some possible associations, but these are necessarily incomplete. A god I've listed as "associated with warfare," for example, was certainly far more than that to their people.

Abnoba
Gaul and Britain. Goddess. Associated with the hunt and the wilderness.

Aengus
Ireland. God. Tuatha de Danann. Also known as Oengus, Aengus Og or Aengus mac Og. Associated with love and inspiration.

Aine
Ireland. Goddess. Tuatha de Danann. Associated with midsummer and sovereignty.

Airmed
Ireland. Goddess. Tuatha de Danann. Associated with herbs and healing.

Alaunus
Gaul (Worship sites in modern-day Austria.) God. Associated with healers and seers.

Alisanos
Gaul (Worship sites in modern-day France.) God. Possibly associated with stone, or the earth.

Ancasta
Britain. (Worship site near Southampton.) Goddess. Possibly associated with the River Itchen.

Andraste
Britain. (Worship sites near Norfolk.) Goddess. Known as a goddess of Boudica's Iceni tribe. Associated with warfare.

Arduinna
Gaul. (Worship sites in the Ardennes.) Goddess. Associated with the wilderness; images show her riding a boar.

Arianhrod
Wales. Goddess. Mother of Dylan and Lleu.

Artio
Gaul. (Worship sites near Bern, Switzerland and in parts of western Germany.)Goddess. Associated with the bear.

Aveta
Gaul. (Worship sites near Trier, Germany.) Goddess. Associated with motherhood.

Be Binn
Ireland. Goddess. Tuatha de Danann. Associated with childbirth and the afterlife.

Belatucadros
Britain. (Worship sites in northern England.) God. Associated with battle.

Belenos

Gaul and Britain. (Worship sites across Europe.) God. Associated with the sun and with healing.

Belisama

Gaul and Britain. (Worship sites in Gaul and northern England.) Goddess. Associated with rivers and lakes; possibly associated with the sun and summer.

Bergusia

Gaul. (Worship site in Alesia.)Goddess. Associated with abundance and/or metalwork. Consort of Ucuetis.

Blodeuwedd

Wales. Goddess. Bride of Lleu Llaw Gyffes, created from flowers.

Boann

Ireland. Goddess. Tuatha de Danann. Mother of Aengus by the Dagda. Associated with the Boyne River.

Borvo

Gaul (Worship sites primarily in northeastern France but spread elsewhere as well.) God. A consort of Damona. Associated with healing.

Bran

Wales. God. Son of Llyr. Associated with leadership.

Branwen
Wales. Goddess. Daughter of Llyr.

Brigantia
Britain. Goddess. A tribal deity; associated with healing and rivers.

Brigid
Ireland. Goddess. Tuatha de Danann. Also known as Brigit, Bride or Brid. Daughter of the Dagda. Associated with poetry, healing and crafts, particularly smithing.

Camulus
Gaul and Britain. (Many worship sites throughout Gaul.) God. Associated with war and battle.

Carantana
Gaul. (Worship site at Etrechy, France.) Goddess. Possibly associated with wisdom; name refers to constancy.

Cernunnos
Gaul. (Worship sites near Paris, France and likely a deity with widespread worship across the region.). God. Associated with nature and commerce.

Cerridwen
Wales. Goddess. Sorceress. Associated with poetry, inspiration and transformation. First attested in the Tale of Taliesin, which may date to the 9th--12th century.

Cliodhna

Ireland. Goddess. Tuatha de Danann. Associated with beauty and love; also associated with the banshee.

Cocidius

Britain. (Worship sites near Hadrian's Wall.) God. Associated with battle and hunting.

Coventina

Britain. (Worship sites near Northumberland.) Goddess. Associated with fresh-water springs and wells.

Creidhne

Ireland. God. Tuatha de Danann. Associated with crafts, specifically goldsmithing. One of the three gods of art, with Luchtaine and Goibniu.

Dagda

Ireland. God. Tuatha de Danann. Father of many gods. Associated with power and plenty, holder of a magical club and a bottomless cauldron.

Damona

Gaul. (Worship sites in eastern France.) Goddess. Sometimes paired with Borvo. Associated with healing springs and spas.

Danu

Ireland. Goddess. Mother of the Tuatha de Danann (People of Danu). Associated with the land.

Dian Cecht

Ireland. God. Tuatha de Danann. Associated with healing.

Donn

Ireland. God. Associated with the dead; considered an ancestor of the Irish people.

Eithne

Ireland. Goddess. Daughter of the Fomorian king Balor. Mother of Lugh.

Epona

Gaul, Germania and Britain. (Worship sites all over Europe, including Rome.) Goddess. Associated with horses (and cavalry), fertility and abundance.

Erecura

Gaul. (Many worship sites in the Danube region.) Goddess. Associated with fertility and the underworld.

Esus

Gaul. (Worship sites in Paris, France and Trier, Germany.) Connected with Taranis and Teutates.

Etain

Ireland. Goddess. Tuatha de Danann. Best known for her role in "The Wooing of Etain." Subject to many transformations.

Etiona

Gaul. (Worship site at Etrechy, France.) Goddess. Possibly associated with knowledge.

Fand

Ireland. Goddess. Tuatha de Danann. Associated with the sea and with the faeries.

Flidais

Ireland. Goddess. Tuatha de Danann. Associated with shapeshifting, cattle and plenty.

Gnatus

Gaul. (Worship site at Etrechy, France.) God. Possibly associated with knowledge.

Goibniu

Ireland. God. Tuatha de Danann. Associated with crafts, specifically smithing. One of the three gods of art, with Creidhne and Luchtaine.

Grannus

Gaul and Germania. (Worship sites in northern Germany and France.) God. Associated with healing springs; in some places associated with the sun.

Gwydion

Wales. God. Brother of Arianhrod, uncle of Lleu. Associated with magic.

Hidua

Gaul. (Worship site at Etrechy, France.) Goddess.
Possibly associated with childbirth.

Isosa

Gaul. (Worship site at Etrechy, France.) Goddess. Name
means "respected one."

Leucetius

Gaul. God. Consort of Nematona.

Lir

Ireland. God. Tuatha de Danann. Associated with the sea.

Lleu

Wales. God. Called "Lleu Llaw Gyffes." Son of Arianhrod.
Associated with battle and magic.

Luchtaine

Ireland. God. Tuatha de Danann. Associated with crafts,
specifically woodworking. One of the three gods of art,
with Goibniu and Creidhne.

Lugh

Ireland. God. Tuatha de Danann. Called "Lugh
Lamhfada" (Lugh of the Long Arm). Master of all art and
craft. Associated with excellence and skill.

Lugus

Gaul. (Worship sites in France including Montmarte; other sites include Galicia in Spain.) God. Associated with animals, and with money.

Mabon

Wales. God. Called Mabon ap Modron. Associated with hunting.

Manannan

Ireland, Isle of Man. God. Tuatha de Danann Called "Manannan mac Lir" (Manannan son of Lir). Associated with the sea and the afterlife.

The Matrones

Gaul and Germania. (Worship sites in northwestern Europe.) Goddess. Triad of goddesses associated with family and fertility.

Medb

Ireland. Goddess. Associated with kingship and intoxication.

Meduna

Gaul. (Worship site near Trier, Germany.) Goddess. Associated with mead, likely associated with kingship.

Modron

Wales. Goddess. Mother of Mabon. Likely associated with motherhood and fertility.

Mogons

Britain and Gaul. Associations uncertain, had Gallic and Roman devotees.

Morrigan

Ireland. Goddess. Tuatha de Danann. Associated with war and kingship.

Mullo

Gaul. (Worship sites in Brittany and Normandy.) God. Associated with healing, particularly of the eyes.

Nantosuelta

Gaul. (Worship sites in the Alsace-Lorraine region.) Goddess. Associated with fertility and prosperity.

Naria

Gaul. (Worship sites in Switzerland.) Goddess. Probably associated with fertility and, perhaps, good fortune.

Nehellenia

Gaul and Germania. (Worship sites in Zeeland in the Netherlands.) Goddess. Uncertain whether her origins are Celtic or Germanic. Associated with sea travel and trade.

Nematona

Gaul and Britain. (Worship sites in Bath, England and Trier, Germany, among others.) Goddess. Tribal deity of the Nemetes; may be associated with sacred places.

Nimue
Wales. Goddess. Associated with lakes and springs.

Nodens
Britain and possibly Gaul. (Worship sites in Gloustershire, Englahd and perhaps Mainz, Germany.) God. Possibly associated with the sea and with hunting.

Nuada
Ireland. God. Tuatha de Danann. Called "Nuada Airgetlamh" (Nuada of the Silver Arm).

Ogma
Ireland. God. Tuatha de Danann. Deviser of the Ogham. Associated with eloquence and wise speech.

Ogmios
Gaul. God. Associated with eloquence and the underworld.

Rhiannon
Wales. Goddess. Associated with kingship and horses.

Ritona
Gaul. (Worship centered in what is now Trier, Germany.) Goddess. Associated with water fords.

Rosmerta

Gaul. (Worship sites in a wide area including France, Germany, Belgium and the Netherlands.) Goddess. Associated with abundance.

Senuna

Britain. (Worship site in North Hertfordshire, discovered in 2002.) Goddess. Likely associated with a spring.

Sequana

Gaul. (Worship sites in the area of the Seine River.) Goddess. Associated with the Seine and with healing.

Sirona

Gaul. (Worship sites in east and central Gaul and along the Danube limes.) Goddess. Sometimes consort of Grannus. Associated with healing.

Sucellus

Gaul. (Worship sites in the Alsace-Lorraine region; one site in York, England.) God. Consort of Nantosuelta. Associated with farming, brewing and winemaking.

Sulis

Britain (Worship site in Bath, England.) Goddess. Associated with healing.

Tailtiu

Ireland. Goddess. Foster mother of Lugh; the festival of Lughnasadh was created by him in her honor. Associated with agriculture. (Would also be a good deity to call on with regard to issues of fosterage.)

Taranis

Gaul and Britain. (Worship sites in Gaul and elsewhere including the Rhine region.) God. Associated with the thunderstorm. Often grouped with Teutates and Esus.

Teutates

Gaul and Britain. (Worship sites widely ranging through Gaul.) God. Associated with defense and protection. Often grouped with Esus and Taranis.

Ucuetis

Gaul. (Worship site in Alesia, Burgundy.) God. Associated with smithing and bronzework. Consort of Bergusia.

Vercana

Gaul (Worship sites at Trier and in Ernstweiler, Germany.) Goddess. Associations are unclear but may have to do with inspiration and healing.

Visucius

Gaul. (Worship sites mainly along the Rhine.) God. Possibly associated with trade.

References

Green, Miranda J. *Dictionary of Celtic Myth and Legend.*
New York: Thames and Hudson, 1992.

Mackillop, James. *Dictionary of Celtic Mythology.* New
York: Oxford University Press, 1998.

Monaghan, Patricia. *The Encyclopedia of Celtic
Mythology and Folklore.* New York: Checkmark
Books, 2004.

The road is never-ending,
the journey ever-blessed.

2242617R00069

Printed in Germany
by Amazon Distribution
GmbH, Leipzig